FAMOUS PEOPLE'S CATS

BY RONNA MOGELON

ST. MARTIN'S PAPERBACKS

For my parents,
Alex and Lila

FAMOUS PEOPLE'S CATS

Copyright © 1995 by Ronna Mogelon.

ISBN: 0-312-95619-3

Printed in the United States of America

St. Martin's Paperbacks edition/September 1995

10 9 8 7 6 5 4 3 2 1

ADAM & EVE'S CAT

CHRISTOPHER COLUMBUS' CAT

SIGMUND FREUD'S CAT

ALBERT EINSTEIN'S CAT

J. EDGAR HOOVER'S CAT

LONE RANGER'S CAT

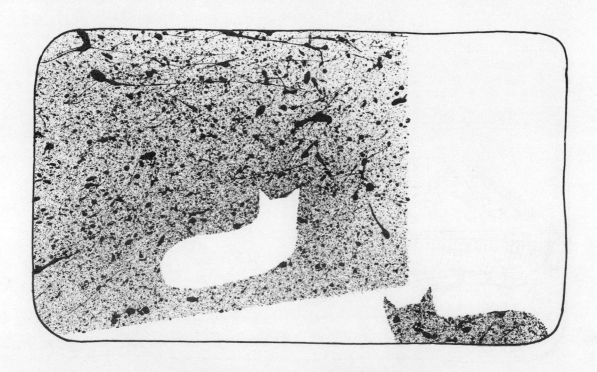

JACKSON POLLOCK'S CAT

NEWT GINGRICH'S CAT

WALT DISNEY'S CAT

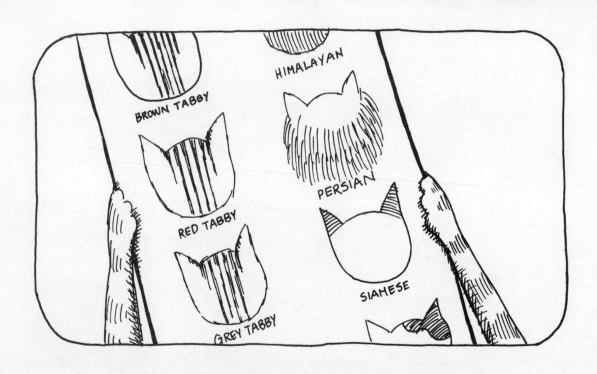

FREDERICK FEKKAI'S CAT

SIR EDMUND HILLARY'S CAT

BOBBY FISCHER'S CATS

DONALD TRUMP'S CAT

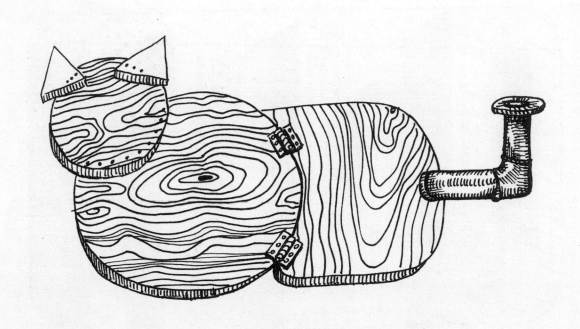

BOB VILA'S CAT

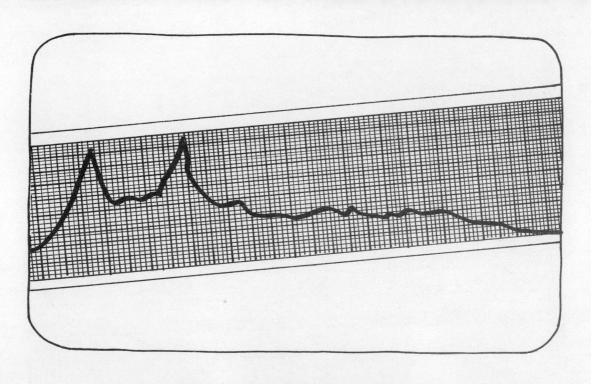

DR. JACK KEVORKIAN'S CAT

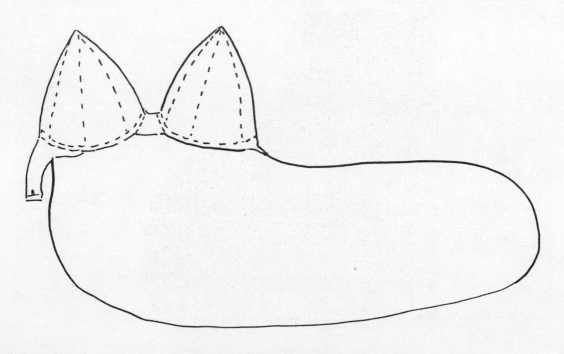

MADONNA'S CAT

GLENN GOULD'S CAT

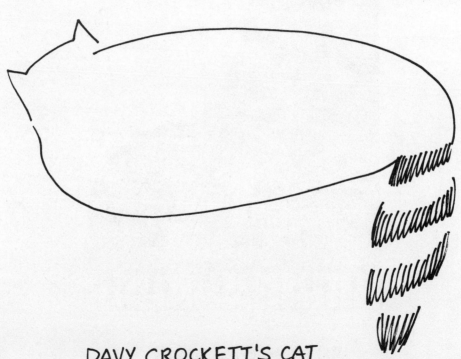

DAVY CROCKETT'S CAT

KING TUT'S CAT

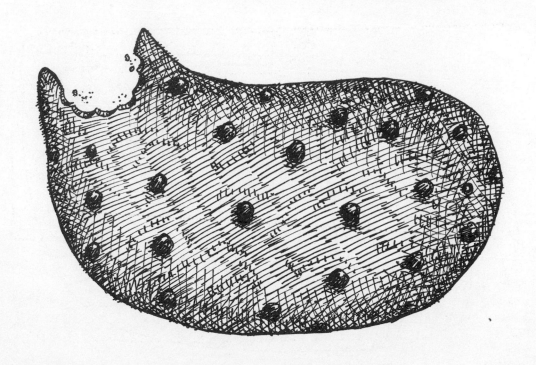

MRS. FIELDS' CAT

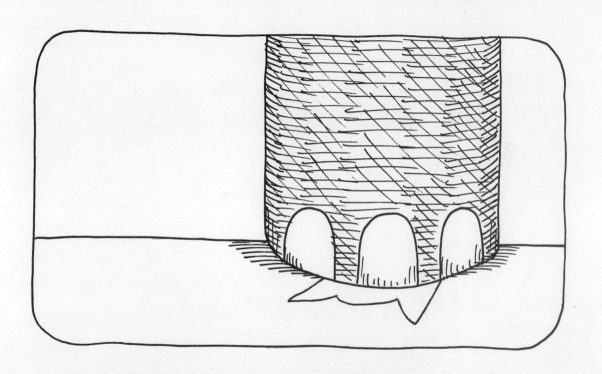

BABAR'S CAT

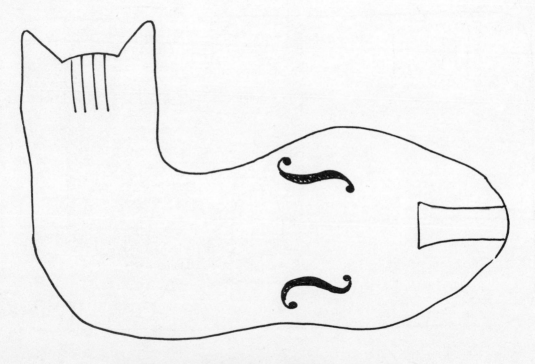

ISAAC STERN'S CAT

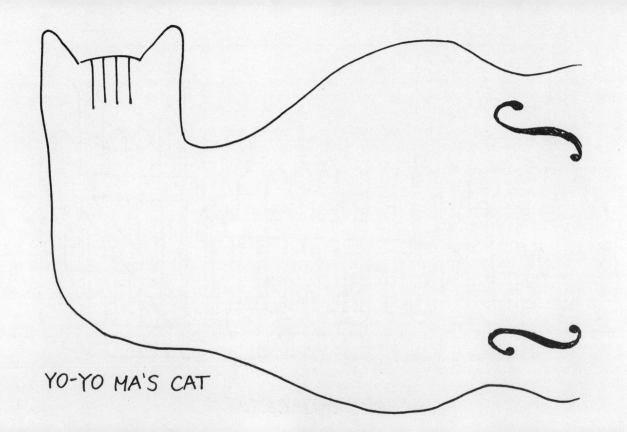

YO-YO MA'S CAT

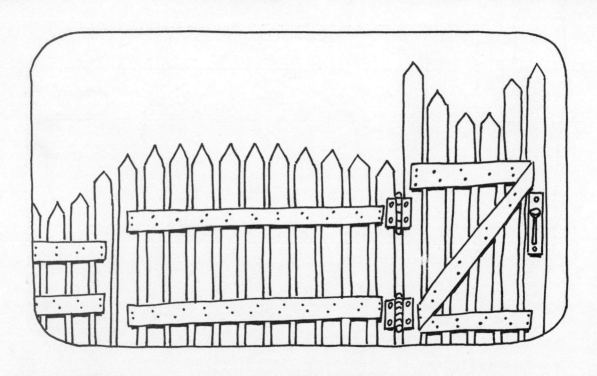

TOM SAWYER'S CAT

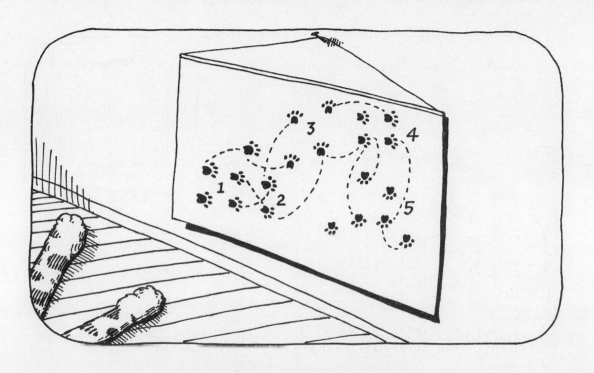

ARTHUR MURRAY'S CAT

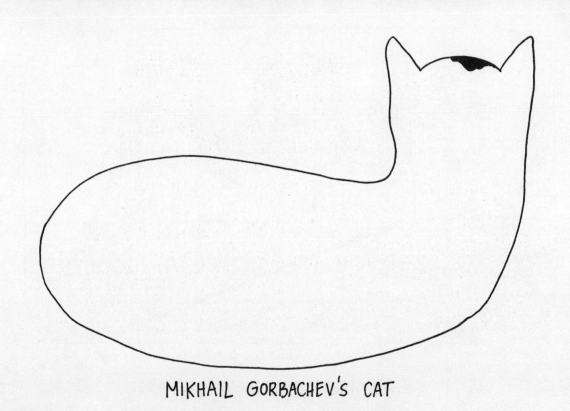

MIKHAIL GORBACHEV'S CAT

FRANK LLOYD WRIGHT'S CAT

TARZAN'S CAT

EDWARD GOREY'S CAT

SALVADOR DALI'S CAT

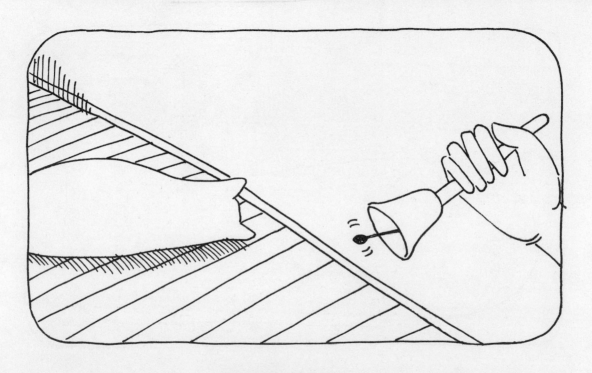

PAVLOV'S CAT

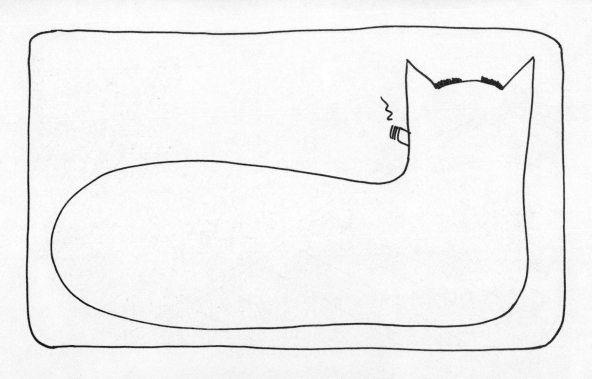

GROUCHO MARX'S CAT

GERTRUDE STEIN'S CAT

BETTY CROCKER'S CAT

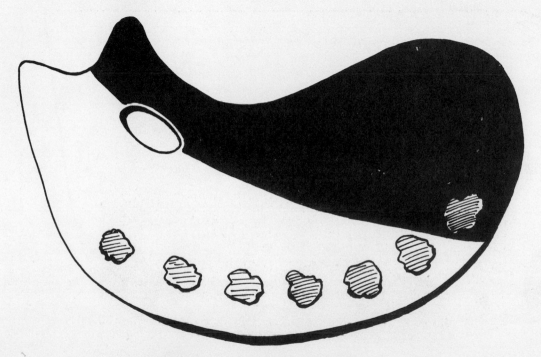

PABLO PICASSO'S CAT

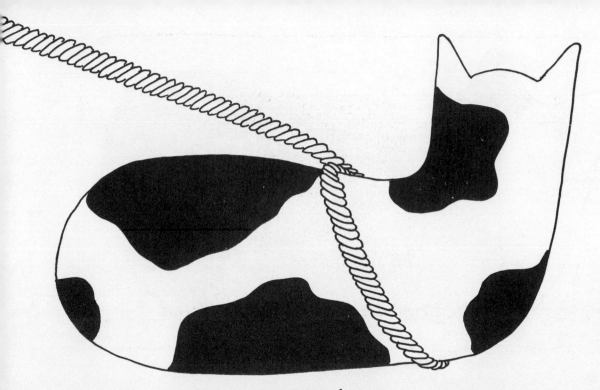

WILL ROGERS' CAT

ANDY WARHOL'S CAT

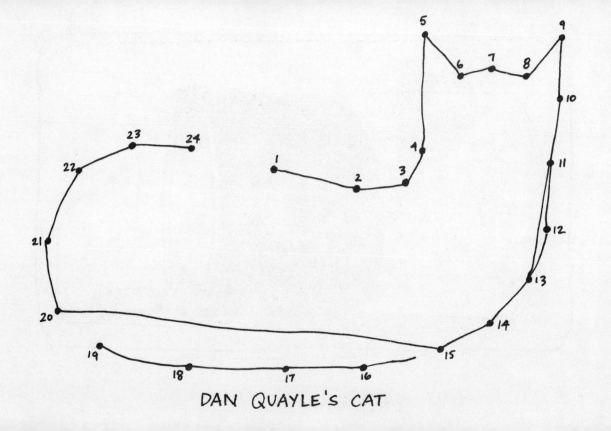

DAN QUAYLE'S CAT

ERTÉ'S CAT

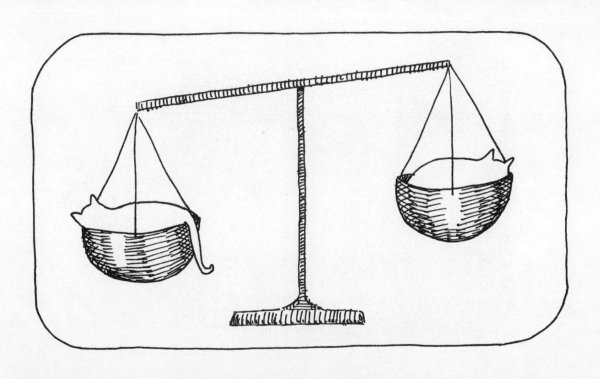

ALAN DERSHOWITZ'S CATS

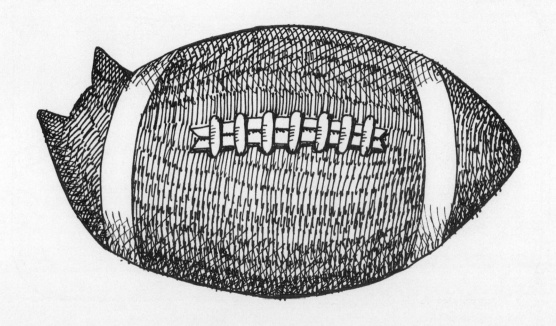

STEVE YOUNG'S CAT

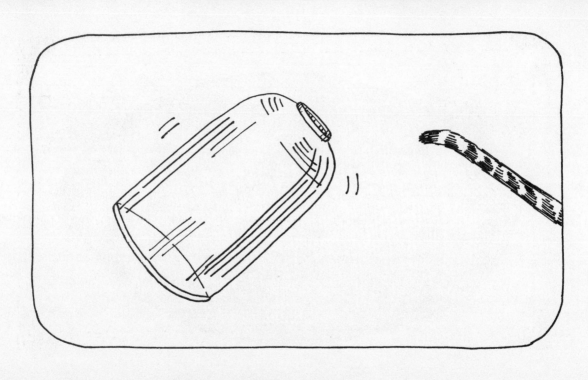

SYLVIA PLATH'S CAT

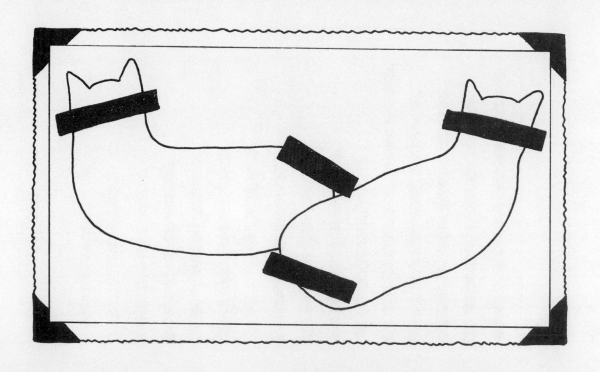

ROBERT MAPPLETHORPE'S CATS

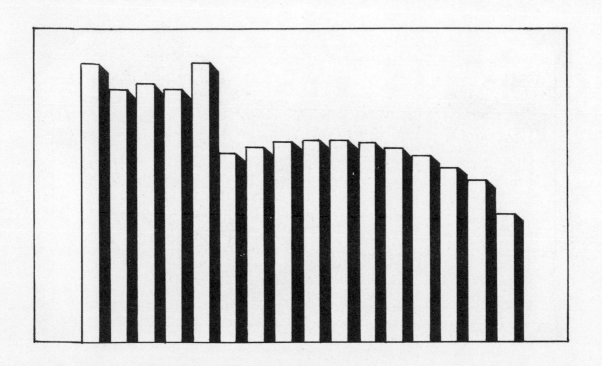

LOUIS RUKEYSER'S CAT

ARNOLD PALMER'S CAT

WALDO'S CAT

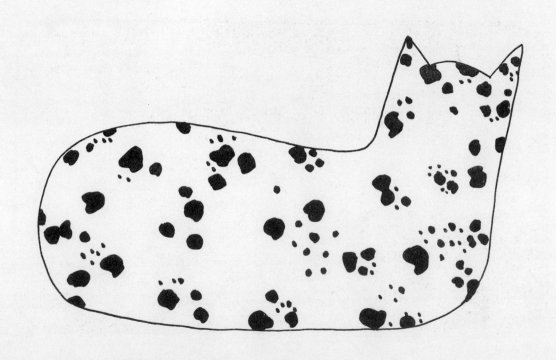

CRUELLA DE VILLE'S CAT

MARTHA STEWART'S CAT

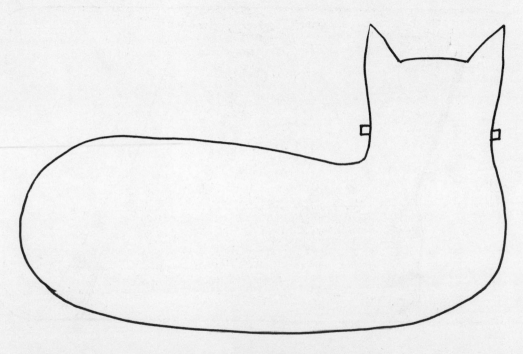

FRANKENSTEIN's CAT

MICHAEL JACKSON'S CAT

PRESIDENT BILL CLINTON'S CAT

MOE'S CAT

NEIL ARMSTRONG'S CAT

MICHAEL BOLTON'S CAT

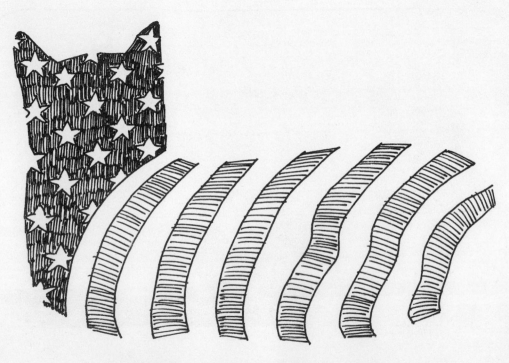

BETSY ROSS' CAT

EDWARD SCISSORHANDS' CATS

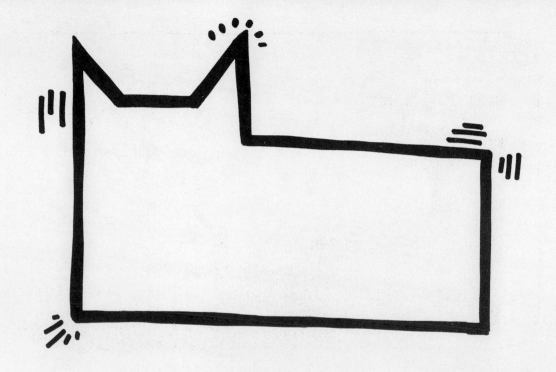

KEITH HARING'S CAT

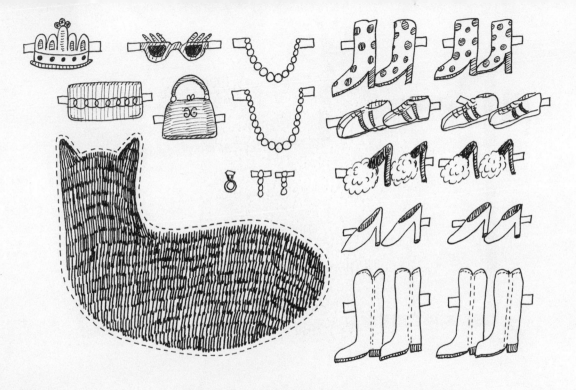

IMELDA MARCOS' CAT

DAVID COPPERFIELD'S CAT

RORSCHACH'S CAT

INVISIBLE MAN'S CAT

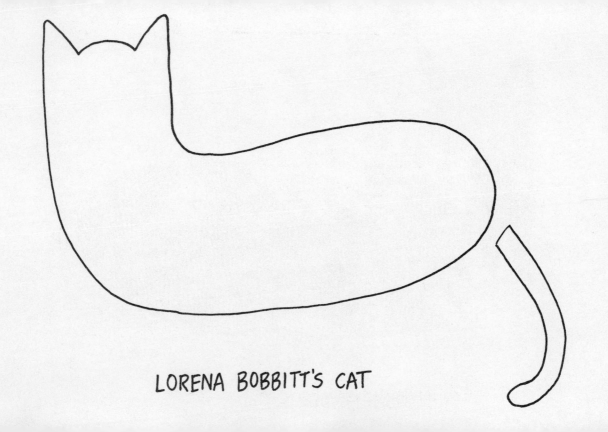

LORENA BOBBITT'S CAT

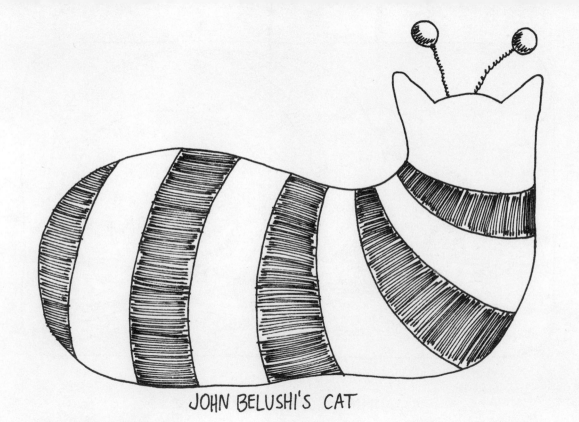

JOHN BELUSHI'S CAT

JIMMY HOFFA'S CAT

JOAN MIRÓ'S CAT

MICHELANGELO'S CATS

SHAQUILLE O'NEAL'S CAT

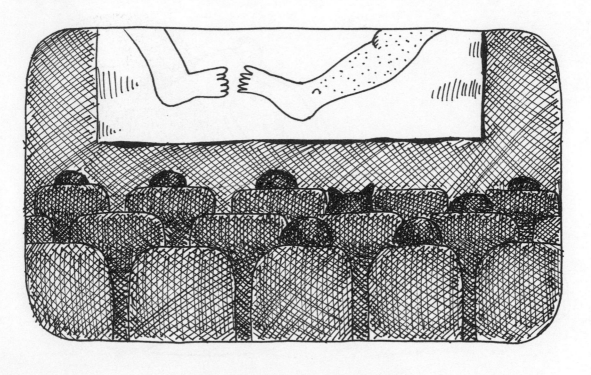

PEE WEE HERMAN'S CAT

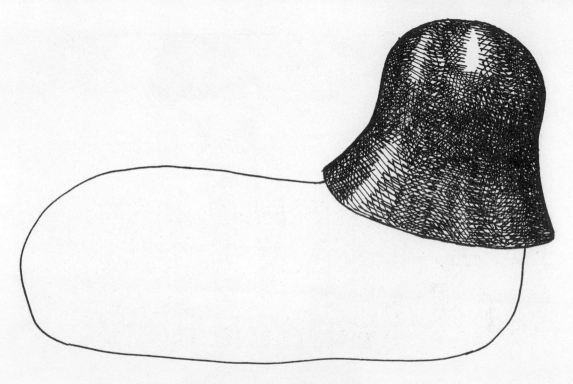

DARTH VADER'S CAT

COLONEL SANDERS' CAT

FRANZ KAFKA'S CAT

RCA VICTOR'S CAT

KING KONG'S CAT

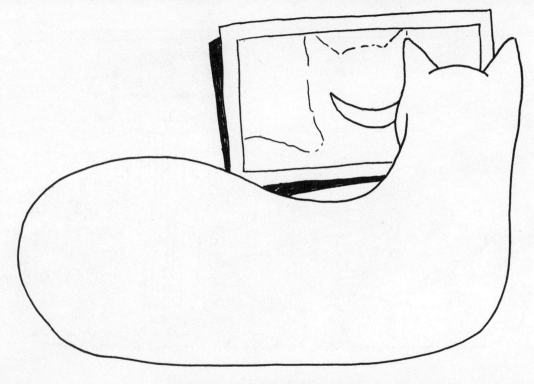

LEWIS CARROLL'S CAT

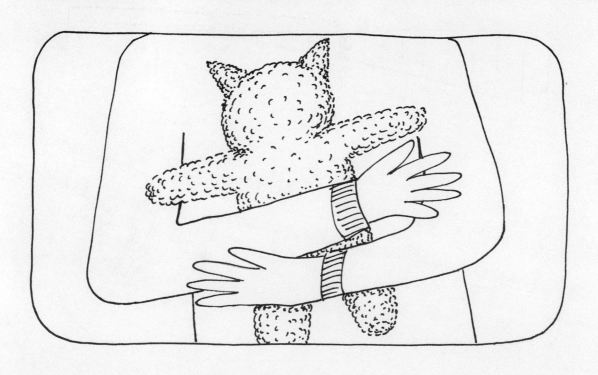

TEDDY ROOSEVELT'S CAT

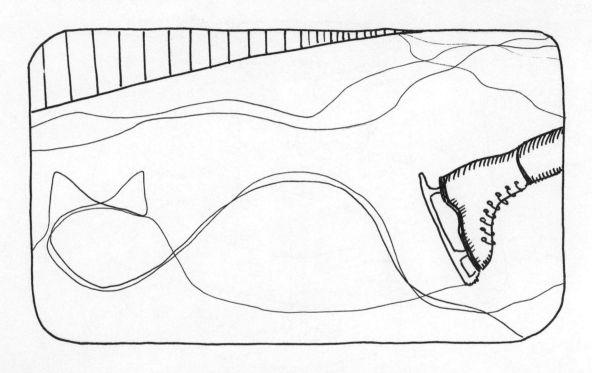

NANCY KERRIGAN'S CAT

JAMES BOND'S CAT

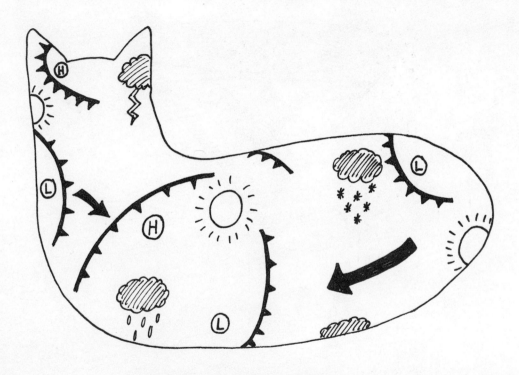

WILLARD SCOTT'S CAT

HUGH HEFNER'S CAT

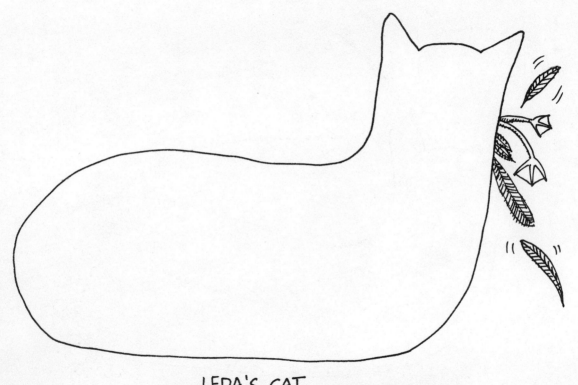

LEDA'S CAT

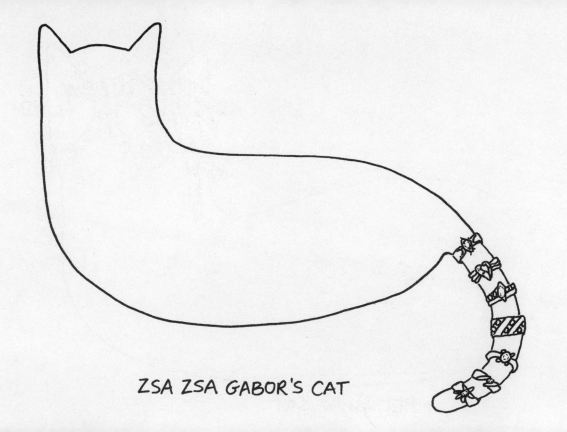

ZSA ZSA GABOR'S CAT

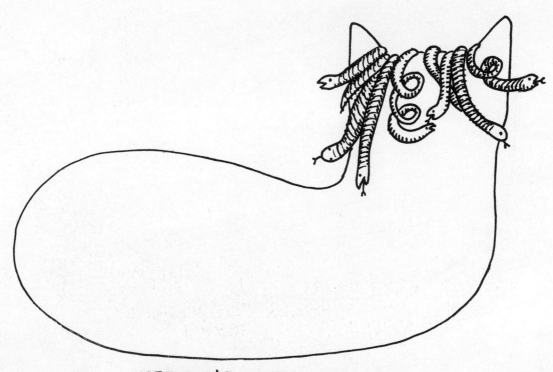

MEDUSA'S CAT

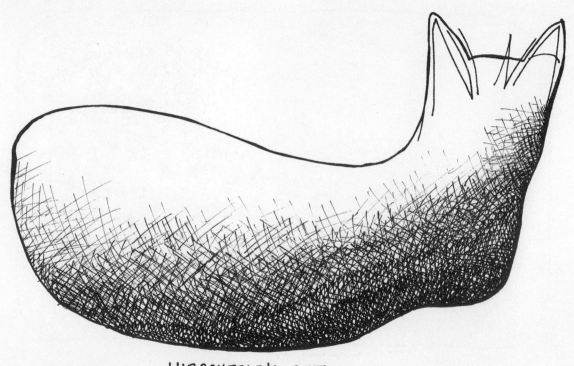

HIRSCHFELD'S CAT

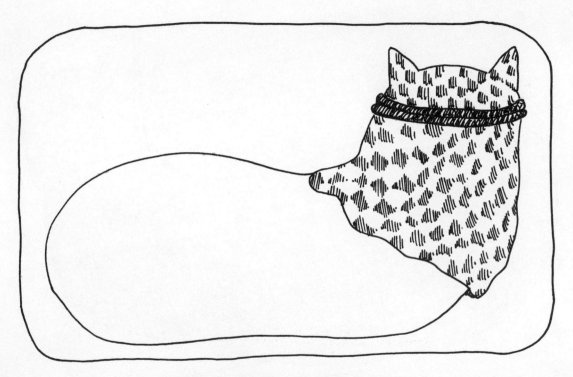

YASIR ARAFAT'S CAT

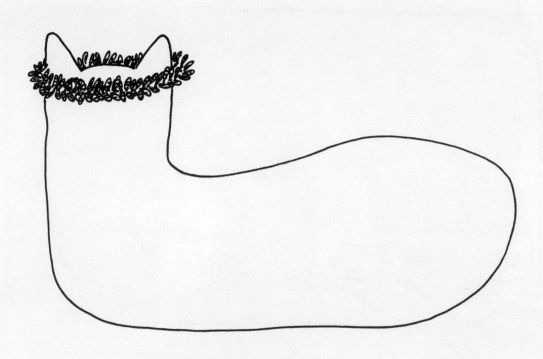

JULIUS CAESAR'S CAT

BORIS YELTSIN'S CAT

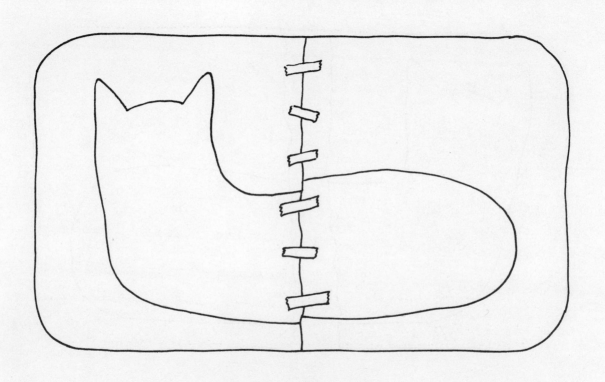

HELMUT KOHL'S CAT

VACLAV HAVEL'S CAT

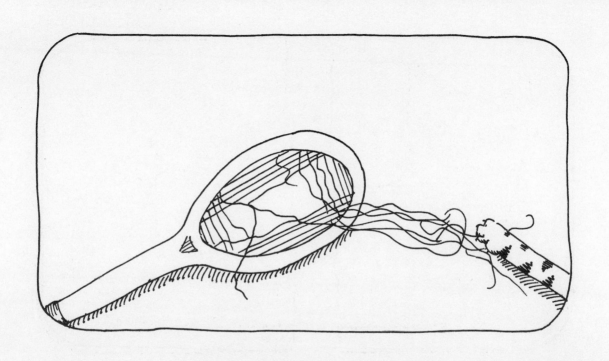

MARTINA NAVRATILOVA'S CAT

SALMAN RUSHDIE'S CAT

WINSTON CHURCHILL'S CAT

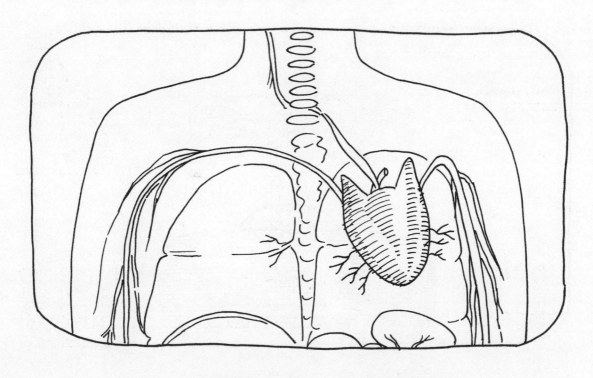

DR. CHRISTIAAN BARNARD'S CAT

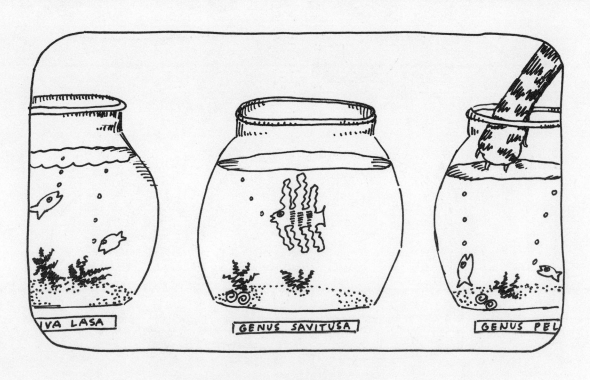

JACQUES COUSTEAU'S CAT

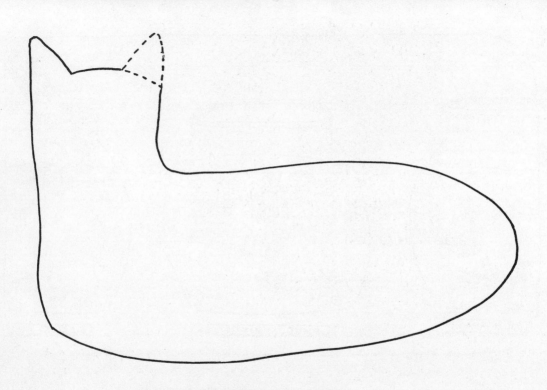

VINCENT VAN GOGH'S CAT